1

TO
PRONOUNCE
SPANISH
CORRECTLY

Stanley W. Connell
Martha Lucía Torres

PASSPORT BOOKS
a division of *NTC Publishing Group*
Lincolnwood, Illinois USA

NOTE ON RECORDED MATERIAL

All references to recorded material on audiocassette
are equally applicable to the compact disc version of
this program.

Published by Passport Books, a division of NTC Publishing Group,
4255 West Touhy Avenue, Lincolnwood (Chicago), Illinois 60646-1975.
© 1990, by NTC Publishing Group. All rights reserved. No part of
this book may be reproduced, stored in a retrieval system, or transmitted
in any form, or by any means, electronic, mechanical, photocopying or
otherwise, without the prior written permission of NTC Publishing Group.
Manufactured in the United States of America.

9 0 ML 9 8

Contents

Introduction

How to Pronounce Spanish Correctly is a comprehensive, self-contained program that will enable you to quickly master the pronunciation of Spanish, including vowels, diphthongs, consonants, stress and intonation patterns.

This unique program is designed for students . . .

- in introductory Spanish classes who need a brief, efficient introduction to the sound system of the language.
- in intermediate and advanced classes who require a short but comprehensive review of the sound patterns of Spanish to improve their pronunciation.
- in self-study programs at any level, where materials must be presented with exceptional clarity.
- who have learned Spanish as their first language, but who also wish to improve their knowledge of its sound patterns and their pronunciation of certain specific sounds.

How to Pronounce Spanish Correctly covers all significant aspects of Spanish pronunciation and consists of this Study Guide plus a convenient audiocassette. The content of the Study Guide and audiocassette has been organized logically and in keeping with sound methodological principles. First you will master the five Spanish vowels. Then you will master the thirteen diphthongs, which most Spanish grammar and pronunciation texts ignore or present superficially. They are important, because, in Spanish, diphthongs occur with such high frequency. Next come the consonants, presented in order from easiest to most challenging. Following these are practical exercises on stress, showing which words and syllables are emphasized in speech. Finally there is a section on intonation, or controlling the tone of your voice when saying Spanish sentences.

The recommended methodology for using these materials is clear and uncomplicated. Simply play the audiocassette, reading silently as you listen to the descriptions of the sounds. Then, still following along in the Study Guide, repeat the words, phrases, and sentences modeled by the native speaker. Rewind the cassette as many times as necessary to learn the materials, and fully master each lesson before going on to the next. Review at regular intervals. The design of the program also permits use of the audiocassette without this Study Guide in circumstances where you can listen but not read—as when driving an automobile. For most students, twenty to thirty minutes is an optimal time period for efficient study. After you have learned to associate the sounds with the letters of the Spanish alphabet, you can continue to use the cassette without the Study Guide.

Learning to pronounce the sounds of another language involves both mental and physical effort. Mentally, you must learn to associate sounds with symbols—in this case, letters of the Spanish alphabet with the sounds they represent. Physically, you must master sounds that often do not exist in English—a task that resembles learning the "fundamentals" of a sport, because it involves coordination and muscular skills. Many of the sound patterns of Spanish closely resemble those of English and will be easy for you to learn and remember. Others contrast strongly, and mastering them will require special effort. All can be pronounced accurately by virtually any student willing to devote the time and energy needed to form good speech habits.

A key concept in preparing this program has been to keep it simple, practical, and *nontechnical*. In describing sounds, the jargon of descriptive linguistics has generally been avoided, and where linguistic terms are used, they are always defined in the text. You will find, for example, that the words *hard* and *soft* are used to identify the *occlusive* and *fricative* consonants. While this may jar the sensibility of the individual with a strong background in articulatory phonetics, most students will welcome it. This program also avoids submitting students to excessively detailed descriptions of secondary and tertiary word and sentence stress, which is better suited to a descriptive grammar than to a work designed for classroom practice. Similarly, several decades of classroom experience have shown the authors that the stress and intonation patterns of Spanish cannot be acquired through complicated linguistic descriptions. Because these tend to discourage most learners, *How to Pronounce Spanish Correctly* presents the key intonation patterns of Spanish simply, without the confusion of musical notes, numbers, squiggly curves, and angular lines that clutter many texts.

Like other languages, Spanish has a number of dialects, both regional and social. The Spanish presented in this program is purposely "neutral" as to regional dialect, and of course represents the speech of educated speakers. For the few consonant sounds that vary from one dialect to another, we demonstrate other pronunciations commonly heard. This practice is kept to a minimum, however, since *How to Pronounce Spanish Correctly* is not intended to be a treatise on Spanish dialectology. It does intend to provide pronunciation standards based on the most widespread and widely accepted pronunciations of American Spanish, without neglecting standard Peninsular features.

The vocabulary used in the examples has been limited to everyday words, avoiding the obscure lexical items authors sometimes use in order to create sound practice drills.

We hope that this brief work will ease the task of students' learning the sound patterns of Spanish, and of teachers' striving to present them clearly. These materials are designed to meet the need for a comprehensive, but not excessively detailed introduction to and review of the sounds of Spanish in language classes. And finally, as you study the sounds of Spanish in words and brief sentences, we ask that you never lose sight of the reality that each word you utter bears a fragment of the cultures of many great peoples. Through your efforts you can achieve the ultimate purpose of second-language study—understanding across cultures.

Part One
Spanish Letters and Sounds

Unit 1

The Vowels a, e, i, o, and u

Spanish has only five vowel letters. All represent simple vowel sounds that you can easily pronounce correctly if you remember some small differences between the vowels of Spanish and English. As you listen and repeat, notice how all of the Spanish vowels that follow are pronounced clearly and rather curtly.

The Letter a

Spanish **a** resembles the *a* in *father*. When you pronounce it, be sure to open your mouth wide.

	EXAMPLES	MEANINGS
Say:	**sal**	salt
	más	more
	mamá	mom
	cama	bed
	lámpara	lamp

The Letter e

English speakers hear the Spanish **e** as two different sounds: one similar to the *a* of English *mate,* the other much like the *e* of English *met;* native Spanish speakers hear these two varieties as a single sound. Most often, Spanish **e** sounds like the *a* of English *mate* /mEYt/, but without the "off-glide" (represented here as /Y/). This **e,** called the **closed e,** occurs when **e** ends syllables or is found in syllables ending in **d, m, n,** or **s.***

Say:	**té**	tea
	de	of, from

---

* An easy way to remember these four letters is to think of the word **demonios** (*demons*), which contains all of them.

bebé	baby
debe	he/she should
usted	you
embajada	embassy
temes	you fear
esperen	wait (command)

The other sound of Spanish **e,** resembling the vowel of English *met,* is called the **open e.** It occurs in contact with trilled **r** or in syllables that end in consonants other than **d, m, n,** or **s.**

Say:	**perro**		dog
	regular		regular
	papel		paper
	perla	(per-la)	pearl
	lección	(lec-ción)	lesson
	acepto	(a-cep-to)	I accept

The Letter i

Spanish **i** has basically the sound of the vowel in English *see* /seeY/, but without the off-glide (shown here as /Y/). Contrast: English *see*; Spanish **sí.**

Say:	**sí**	yes
	lindo,-a	pretty
	amigo,-a	friend
	viví	I lived
	tímido,-a	timid

The Letter o

Pronounce Spanish **o** like the vowel in English *no* /noW/, but without the off-glide (here shown as /W/). Contrast: English *no*; Spanish **no.**

Say:	**yo**	I
	boca	mouth

loco,-a	crazy
poco,-a	little
famoso,-a	famous

The Letter u

Spanish **u** resembles the vowel of English *to* /*tuW*/, but again without the off-glide (here shown as /*W*/). Contrast: English *to*; Spanish **tú**.

Say:	**tú**	you
	mucho,-a	much, a lot
	gusto	gusto, pleasure
	cultura	culture
	música	music

Unit 2_____

The Diphthongs

A **diphthong** is a combination of two vowels forming a single syllable. In Spanish, a diphthong may consist of a **strong vowel** (**a, e,** or **o**) and a **weak vowel** (**i, u,** or **y** ending a word) or of two weak vowels—but never of two strong vowels. Spanish has thirteen commonly-heard diphthongs. As you repeat them, notice how they are pronounced faster and more tensely than similar diphthongs in English.

Say:			
	ai (ay)	**aire, hay**	air, there is (are)
	ei (ey)	**seis, ley**	six, law
	oi (oy)	**oigo, soy**	I hear, I am
	au	**autor**	author
	eu	**deuda**	debt
	ia	**piano**	piano
	ie	**siete**	seven
	io	**serio**	serious
	iu	**viuda**	widow
	ua	**cuatro**	four
	ue	**bueno**	good
	ui (uy)	**cuidado, muy**	care, very
	uo	**cuota**	quota

The Diphthong ai (ay)

This Spanish diphthong is similar to that of the English word *eye*. But note how the Spanish version is quicker, with its weak vowel being much more closed than that of its English counterpart. Contrast: English *eye*; Spanish **hay**.

Say: **aire**   air

4

baile	dance
caigo	I fall
paisaje	landscape
¡ay!	oh!
hay	there is (are)
Paraguay	Paraguay
¡caray!	gosh!

The Diphthong ei (ey)

Again, notice how the Spanish version of this diphthong is faster, with its second vowel more closed than its English equivalent. Contrast: English *pain*; Spanish **peine.**

Say:	**seis**	six
	treinta	thirty
	veinte	twenty
	béisbol	baseball
	aceite	oil
	reina	queen
	rey	king
	ley	law

The Diphthong oi (oy)

This diphthong is again faster, with its weak vowel more closed than that of the English version. Compare: English *boy*; Spanish **voy.**

Say:	**voy**	I go
	soy	I am
	hoy	today
	estoy	I am
	oigo	I hear
	asteroide	asteroid
	coincidencia	coincidence

The Diphthong ui (uy)

Again notice how the closest English equivalent to this diphthong sounds slower, with its weak vowel more open. Compare: English *we*; Spanish **huy.**

Say:		
	cuidado	care
	ruinas	ruins
	ruido	noise
	juicio	judgment
	suicidio	suicide
	construir	to construct
	muy	very
	¡huy!	ouch! wow!

The Diphthong au

Pronounce this diphthong faster and more tensely than its English equivalent. Also, round your lips more on the weak vowel of the Spanish version. Compare: English *howl*; Spanish **jaula.**

Say:		
	aun	still, yet
	aunque	although
	autobús	bus
	autor	author
	ausente	absent
	pausa	pause

The Diphthong eu

This diphthong, while less frequent than some of the others, is found in a number of very common Spanish words. English does not have a similar combination.

Say:		
	Europa	Europe
	europeo,-a	European
	deuda	debt
	amateur	amateur
	neutral	neutral

neurosis	neurosis
neurótico,-a	neurotic

The Diphthong ia

When Spanish **i** occurs before other vowels, it often is so closed that it has the consonantal sound of Spanish **y**. Pronounce this diphthong quickly, and be sure to say it in a single syllable. Compare: English *industrial*; Spanish **industrial**.

Say:

novia	girlfriend
media	stocking
estudiar	to study
viaje	trip
estudiante	student
diablo	devil
hacia	toward
familiar	familiar
demasiado	too
pronunciar	to pronounce
propio,-a	own

The Diphthong ie

This common Spanish diphthong does not exist in English. Pronounce it quickly, as a single syllable.

Say:

bien	well
quien	who(m)
siempre	always
nadie	nobody
tiempo	time
tiene	he/she has
cubierto,-a	covered
conocimientos	knowledge
sobresaliente	outstanding

The Diphthong io

When you say this extremely common diphthong, again be sure to pronounce it quickly, as a single syllable. Contrast: English *studio*; Spanish **estudio.**

Say:

vio	he/she saw
dio	he/she gave
sitio	place
novio	boyfriend
idioma	language
estudio	I study
misterio	mystery
diccionario	dictionary

The Diphthong iu

Though less frequent than other Spanish diphthongs, this one occurs in a number of common words. Again, be sure to say it quickly and as a single syllable.

Say:

ciudad	city
ciudadano,-a	citizen
triunfo	triumph
triunfar	to triumph
viuda,-o	widow(er)
enviudar	to be widowed

The Diphthong ua

When Spanish **u** occurs before other vowels, it is closed and has a consonantal sound much like that of English *w*. Pronounce this diphthong quickly, being sure to say it as a single syllable. Compare: English *actual*; Spanish **actual.**

Say:

¿cuánto?	how much?
cuando	when
agua	water
igual	equal

continuar	to continue
cuarenta	forty
igualmente	equally

The Diphthong ue

This extremely common diphthong sounds much like that of the English word *suede*. Compare: English *suede*; Spanish **sueco**.

Say:

pues	well
bueno,-a	good
cuerpo	body
jueves	Thursday
luego	then
escuela	school
puerta	door
muerte	death
puede	he / she can
cincuenta	fifty

The Diphthong uo

This diphthong occurs in only a few common Spanish words. Avoid breaking it into two syllables. Compare: English *continuous*; Spanish **continuo**.

Say:

continuo,-a	continuous
cuota	quota, payment
antiguo,-a	old, antique, ancient
individuo,-a	individual
superfluo,-a	superfluous
defectuoso,-a	defective
fluorescencia	fluorescence

Unit 3_____

The Consonants ch, f, h, m, n, s, x, and z

All of these consonants represent sounds very similar to sounds found in English. There are a few minor differences, however, which you should find quite easy to master.

The Letter ch
In Spanish, **ch** is considered a single letter of the alphabet; pronounce it a bit more tensely than the *ch* of English *church*.

Say:		
	charla	chat
	cheque	check
	chico,-a	boy, girl
	leche	milk
	muchacho,-a	boy, girl
	chachachá	cha-cha (dance)

The Letter f
The Spanish **f** is also generally pronounced a bit more tensely than the *f* of English *fan*. Say it energetically in these words:

Say:		
	farol	street light, lantern
	fanático,-a	(sports) fan, fanatic
	febrero	February
	afán	eagerness
	infante	infant
	ofender	to offend

The Letter h
Like the *h* of English *honor,* Spanish **h** is always silent. Each of the following words begins with this silent consonant.

Say:	**hola**	hello
	hora	hour
	honor	honor
	humor	humor
	horrible	horrible
	hospital	hospital

The Letter m

Pronounce this sound more tensely—that is, press your lips together harder—than you would for English *m*. Compare: English *map*; Spanish **mapa**.

Say:	**mi**	my
	madre	mother
	mamá	mom
	menos	less
	amamos	we love
	muchísimo,-a	very much

The Letter n

Spanish **n** sounds the same as English *n*.*

Say:	**ni**	neither, nor
	nada	nothing
	mano	hand
	poner	to put, to place
	con	with
	nadaron	they swam

The Letter s

Be sure not to pronounce it with the *z* sound of English *rose*. Also, Spanish **s** is generally less prolonged, so it sounds less "heavy"

---

* However, before certain consonants, **n** takes on characteristics of the consonant that immediately follows it. You will practice this special feature of Spanish—called **nasal assimilation**—in Unit 6.

than English *s*. Compare: English *see*; Spanish **sí**.

Say:		
	sí	yes
	sal	salt
	tesoro	treasure
	desayuno	breakfast
	problemas	problems
	sueños	dreams

The Letter x

The Spanish **x** is generally pronounced as a **gs** sound—with a very soft **g**—or as **ks**.

Say:		
	examen	examination or test
	exacto,-a	exact
	exótico,-a	exotic
	éxito	success

However, when the letter **x** occurs before another consonant, it is generally pronounced as an **s**.*

Say:		
	extraño,-a	strange
	sexto,-a	sixth
	experto,-a	expert
	explicación	explanation
	excursión	excursion

The Letter z

In Latin America, this letter is pronounced as an **s**; in Spain it resembles the *th* of English *think*. First, say these words as you would hear them in Latin America:

Say:		
	zapato	shoe
	zanahoria	carrot

---

* You may also hear the **x** of these words pronounced as **ks**, which is an especially careful or emphatic pronunciation. The **x** of two common words, however, **extra** and **texto** should always be pronounced as **gs** or **ks**; reducing it to an *s* sound is considered "uncultured." In a few proper nouns and words derived from them, **x** is pronounced like Spanish **j**. Examples: **México, Mexicano, Texas, Quixote**.

empezar	to begin
conozco	I know
feliz	happy
audaz	audacious, bold

Now repeat the same words as they are pronounced in most of Spain. Your tongue should not advance forward quite as far as it does when you pronounce English *think*. (Repeat above words.)

Unit 4————————————

The Consonants j, l, ll, ñ, r, and rr

These letters resemble English consonants, but their pronunciation is generally quite different.

The Letter j

In much of Latin America, this letter is pronounced like the English *h* in *house*.

Say:

jugo	juice
jamás	never
mujer	woman
viaje	journey, trip
tarjeta	card
reloj	watch, clock

There are other, "raspy" versions of this sound used in Mexico, much of South America, and Spain. Say these words as they would be spoken in Mexico. (Repeat above words.)

The Letter l

Spanish l sounds quite different than the *l* of English; it is more tense. Mastering it will be a large step toward eliminating your English accent. Compare English *low*; Spanish **lo.**

Say:

la	the
leche	milk
color	color
polvo	powder
real	real, royal
capital	capital

The Letter ll

This letter has a number of pronunciations. The one generally considered "standard" for Latin American Spanish resembles English *y*, but is a bit tenser and more closed. Contrast: English *your*; Spanish **llorar.**

Say:	llorar	to cry, to weep
	llevar	to carry
	llamar	to call
	calle	street
	hallar	to find
	amarillo,-a	yellow

Another common version of the **ll** used in both Spain and Latin America sounds a lot like the *lli* of the English *million.* Let's say the same words using this **ll.** (Repeat above words.)

The Letter ñ

Although Spanish **ñ** resembles the *ny* of English *canyon,* there is a difference. Spanish **ñ** is a single consonant, while English *ny* represents two separate sounds, each belonging to a different syllable. Contrast: English *can-yon*; Spanish **ca-ñón.**

Say:	cañón	canyon, cannon
	niño,-a	child
	año	year
	añadir	to add
	sueño	dream
	compañero,-a	companion

The Letter r

Spanish **r** has two pronunciations, called the **tap** and the **trill.** For the first, simply tap the tip of your tongue against the **alveolar ridge** (the "gum ridge" just above your upper front teeth). The sound, which expresses every "non-initial" occurrence of Spanish **r,** is almost identical to the *tt* of Midwestern English *better* or *letter.*

Say:
pero	but
caro,-a	dear, expensive
hablar	to talk
comer	to eat
gris	gray
triste	sad

The **trill,** used to express initial Spanish **r,** is like the tap, except that it is multiple. Just place the tip of your tongue on the alveolar ridge as you did for the **r** sound of the previous words, and let it vibrate strongly. Always trill the **r** when it is the first letter of a word. The sound is like that often made by children "playing cars."

Say:
ratón	mouse
rata	rat
reloj	watch, clock
río	river
resultado	result
ropa	clothing

The Letter rr

Now that you have practiced the trilled **r** at the beginning of words, you are ready for the **rr,** which has exactly the same sound, but is written as a double **r.** Always trill it.

Say:
perro	dog
carro	car
correcto,-a	correct
horrible	horrible
zorro	fox
ferrocarril	railroad

Contrast the **r** and the **rr** in the following words. Take care not to trill the tapped **r,** for doing so will change the meaning of the word.

Say:	**pero**	but	**perro**	dog
	caro	expensive	**carro**	car
	cero	zero	**cerro**	hill

Now, to really test your skill, say these words; each has both a tap and a trill.

raro,-a	rare
repasar	to review
romper	to tear, to break
carrera	race (competition)
correr	to run
carretera	highway

Unit 5———————————

The Consonants b/v, d, g, c, p, and t

These consonants are pronounced quite differently from the English consonants written with the same letters. Mastering them is essential to speaking correct Spanish.

The Letters b (be larga) and v (ve corta or uve)

Spanish **b** and **v** are pronounced alike. When **initial,** that is, when they occur after a full pause or silence, they sound like English **b,** but with the lips tense. They also have this sound after **m** or **n.**

Say:		
	baile	dance
	burro	donkey
	también	also
	vaca	cow
	voz	voice
	vino	wine
	enviar	to send

In all other positions, **b** and **v** represent a sound that does not exist in English. To produce it, almost close your lips and try to make an English *b* sound. Be sure not to let your lips close completely; they should be quite relaxed.

Say:		
	sabe	he/she knows
	había	there was (were)
	hablar	to speak
	uva	grape
	avión	airplane
	nueve	nine

Here are some words that contain both the "hard" and "soft" Spanish **b** and **v** sounds.

Say: **bobo,-a**   fool

            vivir   to live

            beber   to drink

            buscaba   he/she was looking for

            viajaba   he/she was traveling

            variable   variable

The Letter d

Like **b,** the letter **d** has two distinct sounds. After a full pause or silence, it is a "hard" sound, resembling English *d,* except that the tip of the tongue touches the upper front teeth instead of the **alveolar ridge** (the "gum ridge" above the upper front teeth). Contrast: English *day*; Spanish **de.**

Say: **dar**   to give

            desayuno   breakfast

            dinero   money

            domingo   Sunday

            durante   during

            andar   to go, to walk

            dadnos   give us (*vosotros* command)

            falda   skirt

            dadle   give him/her (*vosotros* command)

Between vowels, or at the end of a word, Spanish **d** is "soft," and pronounced somewhat like the *th* of English *the,* but your tongue should not advance as far as it does for the English sound. Listen to this **d** in very clear, emphatic pronunciation: **lado.**

Say: **lado**   side

            ido   gone

            radio   radio

usted	you
mitad	half
ciudad	city

In popular speech, this "soft" **d** sound is further relaxed, with the tip of the tongue only *approaching* the upper teeth. At the ends of words it nearly or completely disappears, as you will notice when you say these words again, this time without special emphasis. (Repeat above words.)

The Letter g

This letter has three pronunciations. First, there is a "hard" **g,** as in English *good.* This sound occurs after a full pause or silence when **g** is followed by **a, o, u, ue, ui,** or after **n.**

Say:	**gato**	cat
	gordo,-a	fat
	gusto	pleasure
	guerra	war
	guitarra	guitar
	inglés,-esa	English
	angustia	anguish
	ganga	bargain

Second, there is a "soft" variety of this sound, as we also saw in the cases of soft **b** and **d.** It generally occurs between vowels. This is perhaps the most challenging Spanish sound. Pronouncing it properly will considerably reduce your English accent. First listen to the sound in isolation: **g.**

Say:	**agua**	water
	hago	I do
	rogar	to beg
	seguir	to follow
	digo	I say
	juego	game

The third sound of Spanish **g** occurs before **e** or **i**. It is pronounced exactly like Spanish **j**, which you learned in Unit 4. To refresh your memory, in much of Latin America, it is pronounced like the *h* in English *house*; in Mexico, much of South America, and Spain, other "raspy" versions of this sound are used. Here is the easiest version:

Say:

gente	people
general	general
ángel	angel
gimnasia	gymnastics
ginebra	gin
ágil	agile

Now pronounce the "raspy" version. (Repeat above words.)

The Letter c

Pronounce Spanish **c** like the *c* of English *cone,* but without the slight aspiration (puff of air) heard in English. Contrast: English *cone*; Spanish **cono.**

Say:

casa	house
cara	face
coco	coconut
conducta	conduct
cultura	culture
cuento	story

However, before **e** or **i,** pronounce **c** as **s** (Latin America), or like Spanish **z** (Spain). To refresh your memory, this latter pronunciation is like the *th* of English *think,* but your tongue should not advance quite as far. The following words are said twice so that you will become accustomed to both pronunciations. First, the **s** sound:

Say:

centavo	cent
cerca	near
incendio	fire

cinco	five
cielo	sky, heaven
incidente	incident

Now say these words using the *th* sound as in Spain. (Repeat above words.)

The Letter p

The pronunciation of this letter differs from that of English *p* in two ways. First, it is generally more tense, that is, the lips are pressed tightly together. Second, it is not aspirated (pronounced with the slight puff of air heard in English *p*). Contrast: English *part*; Spanish **parte**.

Say:		
	papá	dad
	pera	pear
	pipa	pipe
	popular	popular
	público,-a	public
	propósito	purpose

The Letter t

Spanish **t** also sounds quite different from English *t*. When you say it, the tip of your tongue should touch your upper front teeth, not the alveolar ridge as it does in English. Also, avoid the aspiration heard in English *t*. Contrast: English *two*; Spanish **tú**.

Say:		
	tú	you (familiar)
	también	too, also
	testamento	testament
	título	title
	triste	sad
	interesante	interesting

Unit 6

Special Vowel and Consonant Variations

The Letter y

This letter functions as both a consonant and a vowel in Spanish; sometimes it is called a **semiconsonant** or **semivowel.** As a vowel, that is, when it occurs alone or after another vowel in a **diphthong,** it is pronounced like Spanish **i.**

Say:		
	y	and
	hay	there is, there are
	hoy	today
	ley	law
	estoy	I am
	soy	I am
	doy	I give

The pronunciation of **y** as a consonant varies throughout the Hispanic world. The version you use is not a matter of correctness but of practicality—that is, adapting your speech habits to those of the people with whom you associate. The pronunciation generally taught as "standard" resembles the *y* of English *yes,* but is somewhat "stronger," that is, more closed. Contrast: English *yo-yo*; Spanish **yoyó.**

Say:		
	yo	I
	ya	already, now
	haya	have/has (pres. subjunctive)
	mayo	May
	mayor	major
	oyente	listener

Another pronunciation common in Madrid, Argentina, Uruguay and other parts resembles the consonant of English *joy*. (Repeat above words.)

The Letter n: Special Pronunciations

The pronunciation of Spanish **n** is often changed by the consonant that follows it. For your Spanish to sound natural, you must vary the pronunciation of the **n**. With a bit of practice these changes, called **nasal assimilations,** will become habit.

Recall that the usual pronunciation of both Spanish and English **n** is **alveolar**—the tip of the tongue touches the alveolar ridge. Say these words as a "warm-up," noting where the tip of your tongue touches:

nada	nothing
norte	north
lana	wool
tono	tone
hablan	they speak
duermen	they sleep

But when Spanish **n** comes before **g,** "hard" **c** (sometimes written as **qu**), or **j,** pronounce it like the *-ng* of English *thing*.

Say:		
	tango	tango
	ángulo	angle
	ángel	angel
	ancla	anchor
	aunque	although
	granja	farm
	extranjero,-a	foreigner

This also occurs between words.

Say:		
	un cuadro	a picture
	un gato	a cat
	un joven	a youngster

Before **d** or **t,** Spanish **n** becomes **dental**; that is, the tip of the tongue touches the upper front teeth.

Say: **antes**   before

pantalla   screen (TV or movie)

fantasía   fantasy

donde   where

índice   index

andar   to go, to walk

This too occurs between words.

Say: **un trabajo**   a job

un televisor   a TV set

un día   a day

un dolor   a pain

Before **m, b,** or **v,** the **n** becomes **m.**

Say: **inmenso,-a**   immense

inmediatamente   immediately

sinvergüenza   rascal

This also occurs between words.

Say: **un mes**   a month

un beso   a kiss

un vestido   a dress

In Spain, **n** is interdental when it comes before **z** or the combinations **ce** or **ci.**

Say: **onza**   ounce

danza   dance

sincero,-a   sincere

once   eleven

encima   on top

enciclopedia   encyclopedia

This also occurs between words.

Say:	un centavo	one cent
	un cerdo	a pig
	un círculo	a circle

Loss of s

In many dialects of Spanish, both regional and social, the letter s at the end of syllables is weakened to an aspiration (a sound like English *h*), or even lost completely. In some places this is considered "poor pronunciation" or "lower-class" speech, but in fact there are many countries and regions where it is the standard pronunciation of educated people. Say these words and phrases in which syllable-final s is aspirated:

Say:	calles	streets
	libros	books
	las calles	the streets
	los libros	the books
	estamos	we are

The "Foreign Letters" k and w

These two letters occur only in **loan words**; that is, words brought into Spanish from other languages. The **k** is pronounced like an English *k,* but be sure to avoid aspiration.

Say:	kindergarten	kindergarten (German)
	kilómetro	kilometer (Greek)
	kiosko	kiosk (small booth or stand—Turkish)

The **w** is pronounced like Spanish **b** or **v** between vowels. Relax your lips, but do not close them completely. Let the air escape through them with a bit of friction.

Say:	week-end	weekend
	whisky	whiskey
	Washington	Washington

Unit 7

Special Orthographic Features

Spanish has a special symbol, the **diéresis** (English, *diaeresis*), consisting of two small dots which appear over the letter **u**— hence **ü**. Its meaning is that the **u** is to be pronounced in the combinations **güe, güi,** where it is normally silent and serves only to signal that the **g** is "hard." Say these words that have **gue, gui** combinations without the **diéresis:**

Say:		
	guerra	war
	guerrilla	guerrilla
	guía	guide
	guitarra	guitar

Now say these words, which have these combinations with **diéresis**; pronounce it like an English *w*.

Say:		
	vergüenza	shame
	sinvergüenza	rascal
	cigüeña	stork
	agüero	omen
	averigüe	find out (command)
	lingüista	linguist

The Letter q

This letter always occurs in the combination **qu.** It is pronounced as English *k*, but without the aspiration. Avoid the English pronunciation of **qu** as *kw*. Contrast: English *quit*; Spanish **quitar.**

Say:		
	que	that
	quien	who(m)
	quince	fifteen
	aquel	that

27

poquito	very little
aunque	although

Part Two
Stress and Intonation

Unit 8

Stress in Words and Sentences

Word Stress

In describing spoken language, the term **stress** means loudness. Normally, one syllable of a word or sentence is louder than the others. This syllable is said to have **main stress**. Note which syllable of each of the following words, phrases, and sentences has main stress.

Say:		
	agua	water
	dor**mi**mos	we sleep
	traba**jar**	to work
	¡Hasta **lue**go!	See you later!
	una gran amis**tad**	a great friendship
	Somos a**mi**gos.	We're friends.
	Hablamos a**yer**.	We spoke yesterday.

Syllabification

In order to know which syllable of a Spanish word has main stress, you must first be able to divide Spanish words into syllables. This is quite easy: a Spanish word has as many syllables as it has vowels or diphthongs. A single consonant always goes with the following vowel or diphthong. (Remember that **ch, ll, ñ,** and **rr** are considered to be single consonants.)

a-me-ri-ca-no	American
pá-gi-na	page

continued

cho-co-la-te	chocolate
mu-cha-cha	girl
lle-ga-da	arrival
ca-lle	street
ba-ño	bath
se-ño-ri-ta	Miss, young lady
ca-rro	car
pe-rri-to	puppy

Two consonants within a word are generally divided:

cam-po	countryside
den-tis-ta	dentist
ar-qui-tec-to	architect
im-por-tan-cia	importance

The combination of consonant plus **l** or **r** goes with the following vowel:

a-flo-jar	to loosen
a-fri-ca-no	African
a-pli-car	to apply
a-pre-cio	appreciation
ha-bla-ba	he/she used to speak
ha-brá	there will be
a-tle-ta	athlete
a-tra-sa-do	backward
a-cla-ra	he/she clarifies
a-cró-ba-ta	acrobat
re-gla	ruler
a-gra-de-ce	he/she is grateful
ma-dre	mother

continued

When one or more consonants occur before any of these combinations of consonant plus **l** or **r,** divide before the consonant immediately preceding the **l** or **r:**

cen-tro	downtown
cons-truc-ción	construction
ex-pli-ca-ción	explanation
san-gre	blood
con-flic-to	conflict
in-cri-mi-nar	to incriminate

Two strong vowels (**a, e, o**) together form two syllables:

ma-es-tro	teacher
re-al	real, royal
fe-o	ugly
ro-e-dor	rodent
ca-os	chaos
co-au-tor	coauthor

Diphthongs are never divided:

ai-re	air
deu-da	debt
sie-te	seven
oi-go	I hear
cua-ren-ta	forty

A strong vowel (**a, e, o**) and an accented weak vowel (**í, ú**) form two syllables:

pa-ís	country
a-ta-úd	coffin
bio-lo-gí-a	biology
rí-o	river

continued

he-ro-ís-mo	heroism
con-ti-nú-o	I continue
re-ír	to laugh
rí-e-te	laugh (imperative)

Now that you know how to divide Spanish words into syllables, you can determine which syllable of a word receives the main stress. There are three simple rules; by knowing them, you can properly stress any Spanish word you read, even though you have never seen it before.

1. Words ending in a consonant (except **n** or **s**) have main stress on the last syllable.

Say:		
	ha**blar**	to speak
	ver**dad**	truth
	ca**paz**	capable
	fu**sil**	gun, rifle

2. Words ending in a vowel or **n** or **s** have main stress on the next-to-last syllable.

Say:		
	ca**mi**sa	shirt
	ga**na**ron	they won
	traba**ja**mos	we work

3. Words not governed by the above two rules have a written accent over the vowel of the syllable with main stress.

Say:		
	auto**mó**vil	automobile
	lápiz	pencil
	diplo**má**tico	diplomat
	A**mé**rica	America
	ca**ñón**	canyon, cannon
	des**pués**	afterwards, later

Sentence Stress

You have seen how only one syllable of any Spanish word pronounced in isolation carries a main stress. When you join words together to form a Spanish sentence, only one word of the sentence generally bears main stress. Exceptions to this are sentences in which you wish to show special emphasis or contrast.*

Single-Clause Sentences

In simple Spanish statements and questions, main stress normally falls on the final word. Say the following sentences, placing main stress on the syllable in boldface:

Say:

Enrique es estu**dian**te.
Enrique es**tu**dia.
Enrique estudia **mu**cho.
Enrique estudia espa**ñol.**
Enrique y su hermana estudian en la universi**dad.**
¿Quién vive a**quí?**
¿Dónde vive su fa**mi**lia?
¿Cuándo van a viajar a Ca**ra**cas?
¿Cuál es el motivo de su viaje al extran**je**ro?
¿Usted conoce a Carlos **Ló**pez?
¿Su casa está cerca de a**quí?**
¿Toda su familia va a viajar con us**ted?**
¿Ya se graduaron de la universi**dad?**

Emphatic Sentences

The sentences you have just repeated represent the normal pattern of sentence stress in Spanish. Bear in mind, however, that just as in English, you can change the meaning of a Spanish sentence by using main stress to "highlight" different words.

---

* We refer here, of course, to normal speech, not the stylized language of stage and the media in which main stress is exaggerated and used with unusual frequency in order to hold the listener's attention.

Say the following sentence, noting how its meaning changes when you stress different words.

Say:

Jaime es uno de los mejores amigos de **Juanita**.*
Jaime is one of Juanita's best friends.

Jaime es uno de los mejores amigos de Juanita.
(Highlights Jaime as opposed to someone else.)

Jaime **es** uno de los mejores amigos de Juanita.
(Highlights "is" as opposed to "was.")

Jaime es **uno** de los mejores amigos de Juanita.
(Highlights "one." She has others.)

Jaime es uno de los **mejores** amigos de Juanita.
(Highlights "best." He belongs to a special group.)

Jaime es uno de los mejores **amigos** de Juanita.
(Highlights "friends," as opposed to, say, "acquaintances.")

Sometimes simple sentences have more than one main stress. Examples of this are sentences containing words in a series, contrastive sentences, and choice questions:

A. Words in a Series
Each word in a series receives primary stress.

Say:

Aquí se venden **sombreros, guantes** y **zapatos**.
Here they sell hats, gloves, and shoes.

Los colores de la bandera son **rojo, blanco** y **azul**.
The colors of the flag are red, white, and blue.

Las estaciones son **primavera, verano, otoño** e **invierno**.
The seasons are spring, summer, fall, and winter.

Hay **uno, dos, tres, cuatro, cinco**.
There are one, two, three, four, five.

---

* The normal stress pattern for this statement.

B. Contrastive Sentences

In these sentences, the words in contrast receive main stress.
Say:

No es **inteligente,** sino **estúpido.**
He's not intelligent, but stupid.

Su riqueza no es **material,** sino **espiritual.**
Her wealth is not material, but spiritual.

Dije que **dentro** del escritorio, no **encima.**
I said inside the desk, not on top.

Si uno quiere **recibir** cartas, tiene que **escribirlas.**
If you want to receive letters, you have to write them.

Ella **habla** español, pero no lo **escribe.**
She speaks Spanish, but she doesn't write it.

Te **oigo,** pero no te **veo.**
I hear you, but I don't see you.

No vivimos en una **casa,** sino en un **apartamento.**
We don't live in a house, but in an apartment.

Roberto es mayor que **Juan.**
Roberto is older than Juan.

Esta maleta es más liviana que **ésa.**
This suitcase is lighter than that one.

Sometimes only one of the contrasting words actually occurs in the sentence; the other is implied.
Say:

Tú tienes razón (pero **él** no).
You're right (and he isn't).

Hay **varias** soluciones (y no **una sola**).
There are several solutions (and not just one).

El sabe **pensar** (pero no **actúa**).
He knows how to think (but he doesn't act).

La **señora** es simpática (el **señor** no).
The lady is nice (the gentleman isn't).

Esta es mía (la **otra** no).
This one is mine (not the other one).

C. Choice Questions

In these questions, you ask someone to choose between two or more alternatives. Each alternative has main stress.

Say:

¿Prefieres **té, café** o **leche?**
Do you prefer tea, coffee, or milk?

¿Tiene Ud. una casa **grande, mediana** o **pequeña?**
Do you have a small, medium, or large house?

¿Tiene Miguel el pelo **rubio** o **negro?**
Does Miguel have blond or black hair?

¿**Llamamos** a tu tía o la **visitamos?**
Shall we call your aunt or visit her?

¿Uds. quieren **ver** a José o **hablarle?**
Do you want to see José or talk to him?

¿Compramos **este** disco o **ése?**
Should we buy this record or that one?

D. Multiple-Clause Sentences

Multiple-clause sentences—that is, those with more than one clause—can have fairly complex stress patterns. As a generalization, however, each clause in such a sentence has one main stress.

Say:

María **llegó,** pero Ana no quiso **salir.**
María arrived, but Ana didn't want to leave.

José fue el **único** que no salió **temprano.**
José was the only one who didn't leave early.

Estudiamos **mucho,** pero no lo sabíamos **todo.**
We studied a lot, but we didn't know everything.

Cuando se trata de **matemáticas,** Lola es **brillante.**
When it comes to mathematics, Lola is brilliant.

¿Por qué no comienzas a **estudiar** si tienes tantas **tareas?**
Why don't you start studying, if you have so much homework?

Cuando visitas a tu **tía,** ¿siempre ves **televisión?**
When you visit your aunt, do you always watch television?

Joaquín y Marta **quieren** que tú salgas con **ellos.**
Joaquín and Marta want you to leave with them.

¿Hay alguien **aquí** que sepa **español?**
Is there anybody here who knows Spanish?

Nos vemos **mañana,** con tal que haya **tiempo.**
We'll see each other tomorrow, provided that there's time.

Si se **casan,** van a ser **felices.**
If they get married, they're going to be happy.

Unit 9

Intonation

Intonation refers to the rise and fall of the voice, that is, its tone or pitch. Controlling your intonation when you say a Spanish sentence is as important as using the proper stress pattern, because like stress, tone can change meaning. In this Unit you will practice the intonation patterns of statements, questions, and words in series.

A. Intonation in Statements

When you make a statement in Spanish, it ends with falling intonation.

Say:

Ernesto y Ana son primos.
Ernesto and Ana are cousins.

Guillermo ya se graduó de la universidad.
Guillermo already graduated from the university.

Mi casa está en el norte de la ciudad.
My house is in the northern part of the city.

Viajar en avión es un placer.
Traveling by airplane is a pleasure.

B. Information Questions

An **information question** begins with a question word and requires an answer that provides information beyond just **sí** or **no**. Just as in English, Spanish information questions end with a falling tone. These questions are never mistaken for statements, however, because they always begin with question words.

Say:

¿Cuántos años tiene usted?
How old are you?

¿Cómo se llama su hermana?
What's your sister's name?

¿Desde cuándo viven aquí?
How long have you lived here?

¿Por qué estudias tanto?
Why do you study so much?

¿Dónde encontraste ese vestido?
Where did you find that dress?

¿Quién sabe manejar esta computadora?
Who knows how to run this computer?

C. Sí/No Questions

These questions, which can be answered with a simple **sí** or **no,** end with rising intonation. The rising tone expresses uncertainty; you do not know whether the answer to your question will be **sí** or **no.**

Say:

¿Llegaron Uds. a tiempo?
Did you arrive on time?

¿Juanita es tu hermana?
Juanita is your sister?

¿Hace mucho tiempo que viven aquí?
Have you lived here for a long time?

¿No estudias mucho?
Don't you study much?

¿No encontraste el vestido que buscabas?
Didn't you find the dress you were looking for?

¿Sabe Ud. manejar una computadora?
Do you know how to run a computer?

Interestingly, these same questions can be asked with a falling tone at the end. When you do this, you either know what the person will answer, or are trying to manipulate the answer by assuming "of course you agree with me." Now say the previous questions using this falling pattern. (Repeat above questions.)

D. Tag Questions

Spanish, like English, has **tag questions,** which are brief questions added to the ends of statements. Like other **sí/no** questions, they are generally "genuine" questions ending with a rising tone. Ask these questions using a rising tone:

Say:

Ud. tiene el libro, ¿no?
You have the book, don't you?

Ella va a llegar, ¿verdad?
She's going to arrive, isn't she?

Vamos a ganar el partido, ¿cierto?
We're going to win the game, aren't we?

Now ask these tag questions using a falling tone, which means that you either know the answer, or are trying to manipulate it.

Say:

Me prestas el dinero, ¿no?
You'll lend me the money, right?

Tú compraste el libro, ¿verdad?
You bought the book, didn't you?

Jairo se equivocó, ¿cierto?
Jairo made a mistake, didn't he?

E. Choice Questions

In **choice questions**—which ask someone to choose between two or more alternatives—the tone rises with each choice offered, then falls at the end of the sentence, that is, on the final alternative.

Say:

¿Prefieres té, café o leche?
Do you prefer tea, coffee, or milk?

¿Van a llegar hoy o mañana?
Are they going to arrive today or tomorrow?

¿Prefiere Ud. una casa grande, una mediana o
una pequeña?
Do you prefer a large house, a medium-sized one, or a small
one?

¿Tiene Miguel el pelo rubio o negro?
Does Miguel have blond or black hair?

¿Llamamos a tu tía o la visitamos?
Shall we call your aunt or visit her?

¿Uds. quieren salir o quedarse?
Do you want to leave or stay?

¿Compramos este disco o ése?
Should we buy this record or that one?

F. Words in a Series

In Spanish sentences which feature **listing,** the tone rises for each
item listed, then falls on the final one.

Say:

Quisiera carne, papa y arroz.
I would like meat, potatoes, and rice.

No hace sino trabajar, estudiar y dormir.
He does nothing but work, study, and sleep.

Compré camisas, medias y corbatas.
I bought shirts, stockings, and ties.

Tenemos jugo de naranja, de piña y de tomate.
We have orange, pineapple, and tomato juice.

Me gusta ir al cine, ver televisión y jugar al tenis.
I like to go to the movies, watch television, and play tennis.

Counting is a special type of listing. There are several ways to
count in Spanish. In the most common way, counting at normal
speed, the tone rises on each number, then falls on the last one.

Say:

uno, dos, tres, cuatro, cinco, seis, siete.

Then there is a slow, deliberate way of counting, with a falling tone on every number.

Say:

ocho, nueve, diez, once, doce, trece, catorce.

In a third, very fast way to count, without pauses, you hold the tone level until the last number, where it falls.

Say:

uno dos tres cuatro cinco seis siete.

Part Three
Appendix

The Spanish Alphabet in Sequence

Letter	Name	Key Word(s)	Page
a	a	mamá	1
b	be	baile (hard)	18
		sabe (soft)	18
c	ce	casa (k)	21
		centavo (s/th)	21
ch	che	muchacha	10
d	de	dinero (hard)	19
		lado (soft)	19
e	e	bebé (closed)	1
		papel (open)	2
f	efe	febrero	10
g	ge	gusto (hard)	20
		agua (soft)	20
		gente (h)	21
h	hache	honor	11
i	i	tímido	2
j	jota	mujer	14
k	ka	kilómetro	26
l	ele	color	14
ll	elle	calle	15
m	eme	amamos	11
n	ene	nada	11
		(changes)	24
ñ	eñe	niña	15
o	o	poco	3
p	pe	papá	22
q	cu	que	27

r	ere	pero (tap)	16
		ropa (trill)	16
rr	erre	perro	16
s	ese	sueños	12
		aspirated or lost	26
t	te	triste	22
u	u	cultura	3
		vergüenza (diéresis)	27
v	uve	vaca	18
		nueve (soft)	18
w	doble u	week-end	26
x	equis	examen (gs or ks)	12
		extraño (s)	12
y	i griega, ye	hay (vowel)	23
		yo (consonant)	23
z	zeta	zapato (s/th)	12

Diphthongs

DIPHTHONG	KEY WORD(S)	PAGE
ai (ay)	aire, hay	4
ei (ey)	seis, ley	5
oi (oy)	oigo, soy	5
au	autor	6
eu	deuda	6
ia	piano	7
ie	siete	7
io	serio	8
iu	viuda	8
ua	cuatro	8
ue	bueno	9
ui (uy)	cuidado, muy	6
uo	cuota	9